Also by Kasper Hauser

Weddings of the Times
SkyMaul: Happy Crap You Can Buy from a Plane

Obama's BlackBerry

Kasper Hauser

Rob Baedeker
Dan Klein
James Reichmuth
John Reichmuth

Little, Brown and Company
New York   Boston   London

Little, Brown and Company
Hachette Book Group
237 Park Avenue, New York, NY 10017
Visit our website at www.HachetteBookGroup.com

First Edition: June 2009

Little, Brown and Company is a division of Hachette Book
Group, Inc. The Little, Brown name and logo are trademarks of
Hachette Book Group, Inc.

This book is not endorsed, sponsored, or otherwise
authorized by Research In Motion Limited, the owner of
the *BlackBerry* trademark.

ISBN 978-0-316-07435-3
Library of Congress Control Number 2009927614

10 9 8 7 6 5 4 3 2 1

RRD-IN

Book design by Charles Sutherland

Printed in the United States of America

FROM: Obama for America
TO: Barack Obama
SUBJECT: Hey Barack, the Real Work Has Just Begun

Dear Barack,

With your help, Barack Obama achieved a resounding victory in November, and together we now begin the long journey toward ensuring America's strength and prosperity for future generations.

Barack: are you able to give a one-time donation of $5, $100, or $1,000 to help Barack Obama enable American families to thrive and reclaim their destiny?

Thank you for your continued commitment to Barack Obama, Barack Obama.

David Plouffe
Campaign Manager
Obama for America

FROM: Barack Obama
TO: Obama for America
SUBJECT: RE: The Real Work Has Just Begun

Hey Man,

Can you take me off this list? I can't keep up with the emails — you guys and moveon.org are really clogging up my inbox.

Thanks,
Barack

P.S. Look: Don't take this the wrong way — I'm still thrilled that we won!

Text message to:
Secret Service, Presidential Detail

BarackO: guess where I am?

SecretService: lincoln bedroom.

BarackO: how about now?

SecretService: map room.

BarackO: damn, u guys r good.

BarackO: how about now?

SecretService: china room. are we done with this?

BarackO: k. sorry ☺

FROM: George W. Bush
TO: Barack Obama
SUBJECT: Did my dog show up at your house?

Hey Pardner,

My dog Barney has been missing for the last couple of hours, and I'm wondering if he did one of those "go back to the old house" situations. I know it's far, but he's a quick l'il sum'bitch. Wait, there he is. He's here. He's outside running up right now so . . . Hey there, good boy. Who's my little chunky monkey?

Lauuura? He's back! He just ran up. I wrote to Barack. They hadn't seen him.

K,
W

Text message from:
Joe Biden, Vice President

BidenMyTime: hey u, whatcha doin?

BarackO: m really busy. w/ joint chiefs

BidenMyTime: need me?

BarackO: got it covered. keep working on yr pet project.

BidenMyTime: puppy?

BarackO: universl healthcare.

BidenMyTime: right ☹ can I leave at 4:45?

BarackO: don't care.

BidenMyTime: how does MySpace work?

BarackO: not now. ask malia.

FROM: Bill Clinton
TO: Barack Obama
SUBJECT: Your Middle East Policy Question

Hey Bud,

Sorry for the misleading subject line. Had to get past your spam filter.

CHECK OUT THESE PICS!!! . . .

www.HotGirlsIntoxicatedbyPowerinYourZip Code.com

Incredible — these ladies all live within my zipcode and are single!! I freakin' love the Internet! Kudos to Al Gore!

Later,
B.

Text message from: Ben Bernanke, Federal Reserve Chairman

BernankeB: got a sec?

BarackO: what is it?

BernankeB: what is "compound" interest?

BarackO: u jokng?!

BernankeB: yep. i totally am! ☺

BarackO: k

BernankeB: totally. u think biden is still up?

FROM: Barack Obama
TO: White House Team
SUBJECT: Strategy

Guys,

Our Big Man, Dianne Feinstein, is going to draw a ton of fouls tonight. Practice free throws. And if you can't get the ball to Shaqenstein in the paint, dish it to me or Harry Reid. If they go to Elizabeth Dole, FOUL HARD. See everyone at 5:45.

Yes we can,
Obama

FROM: CIA Director
TO: Barack Obama
SUBJECT: FWD: Intercepted text message

FYI, sir. . . .

>>BernankeB: hey u

>>BidenMyTime: 'sup Bankster?

>>BernankeB: u undrstand "compound" interest?

>>BidenMyTime: ha ha ha ha ha LMFAO!

>>BernankeB: me neither.

>>BidenMyTime: wasn't that the one where the curve looks like a banana?

FROM: Nuclear Command and Control
TO: Barack Obama
SUBJECT: let us know re: nuclear war

Mr. President,

Just wanted to say "hi" from the Nuclear Command and Control System and let you know that we're here for you (Mon. - Fri., between 7:30 a.m. and 10:30 p.m. MST) to kick off a thermonuclear firestorm.

I'm new here, but the management structure is almost identical to Office Depot.

Just give us the signal, and we can have the entire Earth blown up in 1 - 2 business days.

Sincerely,
Darren
Asst. Manager
NCCS

Text message to: Michelle Obama

BarackO: hey hon, we need 2 remind sasha not 2 leave toys in oval office.

FirstLady2U: ?

BarackO: just found tickle me elmo under my desk.

FirstLady2U: not sasha's.

BarackO: ?

FirstLady2U: check tag.

BarackO: "george"

FirstLady2U: i've started a box to mail to laura.

FROM: Arnold Schwarzenegger
TO: Barack Obama
SUBJECT: Let me go after Bin Laden alone

Dear Mr. President,

Listen to me: with a parachute, some Red Bulls and a crossbow I could capture Bin Laden in 24 hours. I could even do it naked. I will grow my hair long for this.

Really, it would be like fighting with a homeless man: so easy. A NURSE COULD BEAT HIM UP. What's the problem?! Drop me in there.

Arnold

Text message to:
White House Grounds and Maintenance Operations

Barack0: i'd like to mow the white house lawn

WHGMO: by yrself?

Barack0: i think it'd be relaxing — riding mower, iPod on, smell the grass

WHGMO: k

Barack0: would love to get a zero-turning-radius rider . . . smthing like the LawnBoy Z3400 HLX . . .

WHGMO: will have to add secret service side-car + gun mounts

Barack0: nice

WHGMO: and a coupla decoy mowers riding around you.

Barack0: fine

WHGMO: also, police mowers to ride out ahead and behind

Barack0: yeah ☹

WHGMO: plus bulletproof glass enclosure for your mower

Barack0: hmm

WHGMO: just like the Pope's lawnmower

Barack0: yeah. let's table it for now

FROM: Abraham Lincoln
TO: Barack Obama
SUBJECT: We watched the inauguration from heaven

Congratulations! We all saw the inauguration on the Internet. They have free wireless up here EVERYWHERE. No passwords for anything. It's really incredible. There is always a really strong signal, and download speed is remarkable. That's probably the biggest difference between heaven and down there — we've just got incredible wireless coverage. Also, it's kind of a sexual free-for-all up here.

Best,
Abe

Text message to: George W. Bush

BarackO: sorry to bother you — what is password for oval office computer?

BushWhackin': there's a computer in there?

BarackO: yeah. apparently u set the password?

BushWhackin': heck, I bet I did do that ☹

BarackO: any ideas?

BushWhackin': i usually just use "password" or my b-day

BarackO: tried those; didn't work

BushWhackin': try "123bored123"

19

BarackO: nope. any other ideas?

BushWhackin': is this a secure connection?

BarackO: yes

BushWhackin': it's "muffdiver"

BarackO: bingo. that worked

20

FROM: Congressman Dennis Kucinich
TO: All U.S. Gov List
SUBJECT: AWESOME LOVE-BUS FOR SALE!!!!

Mahalo! I am selling my 1977 VW bus. This
is a no-worries perfect bus. It has 384k
on the odo and still going strong. It's been
all over the country from when we did the
touring eco-puppet show.

I NEED TO SELL ASAP cuz I need to get a
bunion removed before the peace walk. Tell
me in advance if you want the tires, too, or I
will take them off. First person to test drive
will buy. Great deal at $900. Might trade for
a didgeridoo.

FROM: Sarah Palin <Woof.Killa@
ChristUBetcha.gov>
TO: All U.S. Gov List
SUBJECT: Nigerian $$$ opp!

Hello,

I received an email from, bless her heart, a Princess Vivian who is the daughter of a King of a nation, Nigeria, being under the umbrella of Africa.

As the king's daughter this Princess should have been entitled to royalties from the multi-national oil companies, which I support as a governor of a huge state of Alaska, a huge energy producing state, also.

But what makes me sick is that she, the Princess, could not take the money due to her mother did not bear any male child for him even though she was in a traditional marriage of one man and one woman.

Long story short there is twenty Three Million Five Hundred and Sixty Thousand Dollars (USD56,230,0000.00) in her possession of money that needs to be moved out of the country moving it judiciously to a country such as American with the values that we stand for.

I feel this is money we can accept for the people of Alaska or whatever other states out there are in need of money due to rejecting of the socialist stimulus packet funds.

Hope ta get ta work with ya on this!

Sarah P.

FROM: The Norm and Fran Haldersons
TO: The Obamas
SUBJECT: Let's Get Together

Hi,

We're your neighbors from just down Pennsylvania Ave. We just want to say, Welcome! (The wife tried to bring over an Ambrosia Salad to say "hi," but she was strip searched! ☺)

By the way, could we ask a favor? There is a tree on the southeast edge of your property that blocks our view. It's not a big deal, but could we ask you to trim it?

Sincerely,

The Norm and Fran Haldersons

P.S. Have to ask: Norm's a fit, retired Navy Midshipman and Fran is a healthy housewife with lots of pep. Are you guys into hot-tubbing?

24

Text message from:
Clarence Thomas, Supreme Court Justice

JustClarence: hey

BarackO: hey

JustClarence: u wanna hang out?

BarackO: no

FROM: Her Majesty Queen Elizabeth II
TO: Barack Obama
SUBJECT: A Little Advice

Good Day Mr. President,

Allow me to pass along some useful advice
as you begin your term as a head of state.
If guests are to be served soft-boiled eggs,
give them toastpoints they can really use.
Breaking an egg-yolk with a soggy toastpoint
is like trying to stab a dog with a noodle. IT
IS INFURIATING THAT BAD TOASTPOINTS
HAVE BECOME SO COMMONPLACE.

That issue aside, I wish you Godspeed
and a fruitful and rewarding journey of
leadership. Why do they do it? The sheer
delight of offering your guest a perfect egg is
STOMPED ON AND SULLIED BY SERVANTS

WHO SEE FIT TO GIVE THE GUESTS A TOASTPOINT THAT FLOPS OVER LIKE A PIG'S EAR IN A FILTHY BOG.

One more thing: I enjoyed very much being touched on the back by your wife,

Warm regards,

Her Majesty Queen Elizabeth II

Text message from:
Hillary Clinton, Secretary of State

HBomb: r u still mad about the primary?

BarackO: no, why?

HBomb: why am I flying coach class to zimbabwe?

BarackO: have fun eating pretzels and watching "marley and me" ☺

FROM: Undisclosed Address
TO: BEst OnliNe Pharmcy!!!
SUBJECT: RE: VIAGRA, Cialis, XaNAx!!!! Get anything U want! Safe, effective, discreet. 100% satisfaction guaranteed.!!!!

Hello,

Do you also sell cigarettes? It's hard for me to get them at my job.

I'm interested specifically in Marlboros, Camels, or Commanders. Would also take Harper, Cobra, American Spirit, Drum, Bali Shag, Plug, Merit, Basic, Parliament or Berkley. WILL NOT SMOKE VIRGINIA SLIMS (except Lights 100s).

Also interested in all of the following: Dunhill International Reds, Belomorkanals, Karelia or Karelia Slims, Gauloises, pipe tobacco, or

electronic cigarettes if they could be enjoyed discreetly on a large plane with very tight security.

Overnight? Say 400 cartons?

Sincerely,
"Barry"

P.S. Do you deliver to the Washington Monument?

P.P.S. Do you sell smokeless ashtrays? I'm also interested in purchasing pictures, posters, stamps, drawings or doodles of cigarettes or people smoking or even old cigarette wrappers, empty cartons or packs that still have a good, strong tobacco smell.

FROM: Barack Obama
TO: Oprah Winfrey
SUBJECT: Just checking in ...

Oprah,

Hate to bug you again, but any chance you've got those numbers for me yet?

Barack

FROM: Oprah Winfrey
TO: Barack Obama

Barack,

Sure: Geithner's growth rate of 1.68% per annum is insanely optimistic. Tell the Fed to hold their ground, at least till Tuesday when the Consumer Price Index comes out.

And tell China to take a chill pill — they should be the last country lecturing us on money supply.

Oprah

FROM: Barack Obama
TO: Oprah Winfrey

Oprah,

OK. Can we keep this our little secret?

Thanks again,
Barack

P.S. When you get a chance, the center-right is bugging me for a credible anti-Taliban strategy.

FROM: Oprah Winfrey
TO: Barack Obama

Barack,

Your secret is safe with me. And regarding Taliban policy, you know what they say:

تا زمانیکه ککنار باشد، طالبان وجود خواهند داشت.

(As long as there are opium poppies, there will be Taliban.) ☺

But I'll put something together after my octuplets episode.

Winfrey

FROM: John McCain
TO: Barack Obama
SUBJECT: computer message from John McCain via computer

Barack,

This is Senator John McCain. (My granddaughter is typing this message 4 me).

I am sorry for some of the stuff I said about you during the campaign. My granddaughter loves you and wishes *you* were her grandpa. What are you typing? Stop typing! How does that thing work? Do you just type it all in there and then mail it to Barack? Come back here!

FROM: Abraham Lincoln
TO: Barack Obama
SUBJECT: Charlotte Bronte Showed Me Her Ankles!

It was hot.

Best,
Abe

FROM: Ólafur Grímsson, President of Iceland
TO: Barack Obama
SUBJECT: Huge Sale on Iceland! Major Discounts!

Dear Mr. President Obama,

It's a magical time to buy in Iceland, THAT'S FOR SURE! Our banks are totally f*&@#g *skipreika* and so we got a big sale and everything must go! All the buildings, all the navy and the militaries, even Björk.

Ping me,
Ólafur

P.S. These real Icelandic Navy boots also for sale. Make offer.

1 Attachment: Iceland_navy_boots.jpg

FROM: Barack Obama
TO: Ólafur Grímsson

Dear President Grímsson,

Put us down for your Navy, Björk, and 500 cartons of cigarettes. I think we're going to have to pass on the boots.

Sincerely,
Barack Obama

FROM: Sean Penn
TO: Barack Obama
SUBJECT: Do You Like Me?

I am trying to make a quick list of people who like me — it's for my scrapbook that I'm making.

Please reply ASAP — so far, people have been pretty busy this morning.

Namaste,
Sean

"Sean Penn is . . . an acting virtuoso."
— *Rolling Stone* magazine

FROM: acoulter7648@aol.com
TO: Barack Obama
SUBJECT: Your secret admirer!

You don't know who this is, and you NEVER would think how much I like you and think you are SO CUTE, ohmigod. Guess where I am? At. The TGI FRIDAY'S!!!!. My ffavorite favorite favorite!

My phon is ringing, hang on . . . I'm back. Bill O'Reilly! Is comingg down here! Whoops. That's a free hint! You are so great. Why are there drinks so small? Did I already write you? There's NO goodlooking guys here. Oh I am going to boot.

XOXOX
Kisses
Secret Admirer
I love you

K, I booted, and now I'm rallying :)

FROM: acoulter7648@aol.com
TO: Barack Obama
SUBJECT: self portrait from TGIFs!!

8 applitinis and im'm not even buzzed!!!

i'm gonna come by whitehouse 2night?!

📎 1 Attachment, 323 KB: hi_barack!.jpg

FROM: Prince
TO: Barack Obama
SUBJECT: Keep Me in Mind for Next Inauguration

Congratulations on your election. You are doing a great job.

I wanted to talk to you about an idea I had for the 2012 inauguration:

I come out from behind a curtain made of butterflies. I've got a 10-foot guitar extending from my crotch. I wrap my tongue around the Lincoln Bible, pass it to the Chief Justice with my tongue and then say to him something like, "Ooh, you nasty, nasty freak."

Then I break my celibacy by making love to America, the other justices, and Yo-Yo Ma.

Prince

43

FROM: YouTube Service
TO: Barack Obama
SUBJECT: Recent comments on your video:
"State of the Union Address"

RushLimBomb: lame

FineStein: OMG! he's so cute. U r lame

NewtGrnch: fake.

HuffingTonsO'Fun: yay

BirdInTheHannity: gay!!!

ArnoldSchwarz47: Ja ja ja.

McCain2008: LOL stupid comments

PomPomPalin: OMG . . . what?

XXX_GIRRLS: take a look at my hot pics at
XXX-crazzy.girls.com

Text message from: Michelle Obama

FirstLady2U: hey pumpski — did u notice tracks in snow around kids' new jungle gym?

BarackO: no

FirstLady2U: looks like some kind of big animal might have been poking around last nite?

BarackO: K. will go chk it out

FirstLady2U: thx ☺

BarackO: not an animal — size 12 florsheim wingtips

FirstLady2U: newt gingrich?

45

BarackO: ann coulter

FirstLady2U: weird

BarackO: lady wants to have a little fun on the jungle gym at night it's not gonna kill us

FROM: Otmar Hasler, Prime Minister of Liechtenstein
TO: President Obama
SUBJECT: Greetings Fellow World Leader!

Hello President Obama,

Just a friendly email to say "hello," and welcome to the brotherhood of world leaders. May I call you Barack?

We are all in this together! I face many of the same challenges as you, even as a prime minister of a landlocked alpine microstate!

Let's trade ideas!

Otmar
Prime Minister of Liechtenstein

FROM: No_Hasler@yahoo.com
TO: Barack Obama
SUBJECT: Did you receive my email?

Hello,

It's me again, Otmar, Prime Minister of Liechtenstein?

Have not heard back from you re: my "hello" email (maybe caught in your spam folder?) so I thought I'd write from my personal account. Just hit "reply" so I can add you to my address book. ☺

Thanks,
Otmar

P.S. Are you on Facebook? I want to set up a World Leader group. Could be fun/useful.

Text message from:
Otmar Hasler, Prime Minister of Liechtenstein

Otmar: hello? Is txtng better 4 u?

Otmar: i know u r busy

Otmar: u think i am *not* busy?

Otmar: . . . & i am a legit world leader so

Otmar: you can google me to confirm

Otmar: wd it be 2 hard 2 just reply so i know u read this?

Otmar: BARACK?!?!

Otmar: you just bought yrself a 40% tariff on cuckoo clocks, a-höle.

FROM: Evite
TO: Barack Obama
SUBJECT: Mahmoud is Turning 53!!

Hi Folks,

This is Kelly, Mahmoud Ahmadinejad's (sp?) girlfriend! I know this is late notice but I am throwing a surprise party for Mahmoud!

The theme is cowboy/western/Las Vegas, so get crazy and everyone has to wear a crazy cowboy party hat. We are going to start at 6:30 on Friday at a cool club called Barzoon for drinks and tapas, then we are going to a comedy club, GoatNutz, 'til ?? a.m.

<u>Replies for Mahmoud's 53rd B-day
Hoedown . . .</u>

Yes (4)
Pres. Assad +1 (awesome stuff, thanks Kelly)
Hugo Chavez (hey old man!
Baahhhhhhhhhhh!)
Kim Jong-il +1 (What ya say there
partner!!!!!! Howdy Doody!)

No: (118) List condensed, click <u>here</u> to see
more.

Angela Merkel (Scheiße! I have pilates)
Gordon Brown (chuffed, but shagged out)
King Juan Carlos (dog sitter bailed on us ☹)
Benjamin Netanyahu (F*&* U)

Maybe: (2)
Vladimir Putin (Going try to swing by)
Osama Bin Laden (If I can get away, may
meet you folks at goatnutz)

Text message from: Bill Clinton

WildBill: hey barack!

BarackO: hey bill whats up?

WildBill: can u send Hillary to China next week?

BarackO: ?

WildBill: i'm putting together a surprise party and need her outta house

BarackO: her birthday?

WildBill: no, i'm trying 2 surprise MYSELF

BarackO: ?

WildBill: www. SurpriseYourselfWithHowManyHot SinglesYouCanMeetFromYourZipCode.com

FROM: NYTimes.com
TO: Barack Obama
SUBJECT: My Alerts: Articles in the New York Times containing the terms "Obama" **and** "sexy master statesman"

June 1, 2009 Compiled: 12:52 AM
U.S. / POLITICS

There were no articles containing the terms **"Obama"** and **"sexy master statesman"**

About This E-mail:
You received this e-mail because you signed up for NYTimes.com's My Alerts automated search tool. Your alerts are set for HOURLY.

The New York Times Company

Text message from: Madonna

MaterialGrrl: heard your aunt might be deported

BarackO: sensitive issue, can't discuss

MaterialGrrl: any chance she's up for adoption?

FROM: Kim Jong-il
TO: All World Leaders
SUBJECT: A nickname for me please!

To everybody,

My whole life I want a nickname. Especially I like American nickname like "Scarface," "Complete Bitch," and "the Boston Strangler." Other good nickname is putting "the Kid" after your regular name which would be "Kim Jong the Kid."

Hey come on now don't make me pick my own nickname. ☺ hint: I like animal nickname like "The Cobra", "Catwoman," "Mr. Bojangles," and so on.

Also, no Wizard of Oz like "Kim Jong the Witch is Dead."

Other than that. . . . Surprise me!

55

Text message to: Michelle Obama

BarackO: have you seen my spock ears?

FirstLady2U: oh no.

BarackO: come on, i feel naked w/o them.

FirstLady2U: we said not in public?

BarackO: not public: big mtng w/Putin.

FirstLady2U: spock ears = in garbage.

BarackO: k. do we have some play-doh and a hair dryer?

FROM: Angela Merkel, Chancellor of Germany
TO: All World Leaders
SUBJECT: I don't hate backrubs!

Guten Tag,

I just wanted to clear something up: I DO NOT HATE BACK RUBS!

It just depends on circumstances — where/who, etc.

There are some presidents who could give me a backrub at a G8 meeting or even neck rubs or rubbing fingers through hair. I DO NOT HAVE A RULE AGAINST THAT.

So lighten up! Germans are very sensual people. I am a person and I need to be touched.

Angela

57

FROM: Congressman Dennis Kucinich
TO: All U.S. Gov List
SUBJECT: L@@K: >>>LOVE-BUS PRICE REDUCTION!<<<

OK, some people flamed me for misstating the condition of my bus. Since then, I patched the front with some Bondo and I repainted the whole bus with house paint. You can no longer tell that my sister-in-law's malamute tried to chew its way through the passenger door. It starts fine if you just spray some Binaca into the left carb.

I also replaced the heater hose and got rid of the oil and rabbit smell. This bus is now officially PERFECT. SO STOP FLAMING ME.

Text message from: Bill Clinton

WildBill: did u c the news?

BarackO: ?

WildBill: things heating up in syria

BarackO: i'm not sending hillary

WildBill: shez driving me nutz — I have 2 party

BarackO: not my prob

FROM: Mahmoud Ahmadinejad, President of Iran
TO: Barack Obama
SUBJECT: Guess Who?

No! It's President Me, From Iran! Amadeenajud (sp?). Guess who just got birthday present of new curly boots to go with my cape! Ha ha ha ha. They won't laugh at me again when I give a big speech at the U.N.!

Khoda hafez, goat butt — It's Mahmoud time!!

Sincerely,
Mahmoud the Dude

Sent from my TI-99 Handheld Personal Computer

FROM: Abraham Lincoln
TO: Barack Obama
SUBJECT: Guess who's been French Kissing Marie Curie!?

ME.

end of message

Text message from: Rahm Emanuel, Chief of Staff

Rahm: did u wear your f#$@# spock ears to putin meeting?!

BarackO: no

Rahm: thank god

BarackO: made new ones from play-doh

Rahm: R U F&^% NUTS!?!?!

BarackO: live long and prosper

FROM: Nuclear Command and Control
TO: Barack Obama
SUBJECT: Got Your Hint to Blow Up World

Mr. President,

Mark from swing shift thought you issued the launch code on TV just now, but I wanted to double check:

He says we're supposed to launch if you say the word "look" more than 28 times in one speech.

I thought the code was "foxtrot, echo, muppet, slurpee."

Who's right?

Please get back to us ASAP.

Thanks,

Darren
NCCS

FROM: Sean Penn
TO: All U.S. Media List, All U.S. Gov List
CC: Barack Obama
SUBJECT: Would an "A-hole" go to Mogadishu?

I don't think so.

I am going to Mogadishu on Tuesday to broker a peace deal for us all.

How many "A-holes" can say that?

Sean

"Sean Penn is . . . an acting virtuoso."
— *Rolling Stone* magazine

Text message to: Brian Cowen, Irish Prime Minister

BarackO: thx for visiting white house

BrianCowen: yep

BarackO: did you enjoy your visit?

BrianCowen: sure

BarackO: everything cool?

BrianCowen: real cute to make the fountain green & serve green champagne

BarackO: for st. patricks day. it was meant 2 B a sign of respect

BrianCowen: am I some kinda FECKIN' LEPRECHAUN to you, is that it?

67

BarackO: whoa

BrianCowen: cute li'l Irish fellow, "always happy, dancin' a jig"?

BarackO: wow. sorry — I did not see this one coming.

BrianCowen: may the cat eat you, and may the devil eat the cat

FROM: Malia Obama
TO: Democratic Party Group List
SUBJECT: Help with My School Essay

Hello Everyone,

Could you help me with my essay assignment?

We are supposed to write an essay for our class about how adults learned from their mistakes. Could you please share any funny stories about mistakes you made, especially things you would not say in public. (If you broke the law my teacher said it's OK to say so ☺)

Strictly confidential and anonymous!

Malia Obama

FROM: Jimmy Carter
TO: Malia Obama
CC: Democratic Party Group List
SUBJECT: RE: Help with My School Essay

Malia,

Well this is a funny one. I have lusted in my heart about a person — about that naughty little tramp Barbara Walters.

Good luck with your project!

President Carter

Jimmy Carter, "one of the most successful ex-presidents in U.S. history" — Wikipedia.com

FROM: Barack Obama
TO: Democratic Party Group List
SUBJECT: URGENT. Do not respond to email from "Malia"

Please delete immediately. It appears that Karl Rove has hacked into my daughter's email account.

Regards,
Barack

FROM: Bill Cosby
TO: Barack Obama
SUBJECT: Pants!?!?!?

Barack,

First of all, congratulations. You have made me very proud. Also, what is going on with the young black men today with the pants halfway down?

Sincerely,
Bill Cosby

FROM: Barack Obama
TO: Bill Cosby

Dear Dr. Cosby,

Thanks very much for the kind words. As you may know, I'm not a fan of the "pants halfway down" fad, either.

Sincerely,
Barack

FROM: Bill Cosby
TO: Barack Obama

Barack,

Well, 'cause you see with the pants halfway down that means that the butt is uncovered by the pants. And the pants are saying "what are we doing down here?"

And the belt is saying, "I do not know." And the pants are down and you're just walkin' and there's nothin' but air, see! Nothin' but air between the butt and the rest of the world.

Bill

FROM: Barack Obama
TO: Bill Cosby

Except for underwear. But you've got me laughing here, Bill. I couldn't agree more.

Barack

FROM: Bill Cosby
TO: Barack Obama

And you know who breathes that air? DO YOU KNOW who breathes that air with the pants down and the butt right there? Me.

Cosby

FROM: Barack Obama
TO: Bill Cosby

Right. Bravo. Great bit, really. Gotta run.

Barack

FROM: Bill Cosby
TO: Barack Obama

Do you think God ever loses the TV remote?

Bill

FROM: Barack Obama
TO: Bill Cosby

Wish I could chat more.

B.O.

FROM: Bill Cosby
TO: Barack Obama

"HAVE YOU SEEN THE CHANNEL CHANGER?"

"No, dear."

Thunder! Lightning! Volcanoes!

Bill

FROM: Barack Obama
TO: Bill Cosby

OUT OF OFFICE AUTO REPLY

President Barack Obama is out of the office.

If you need immediate assistance, please contact Joe Biden at JoeyVP@usa.gov (cell: 202.456.1414. home: 202.456.1111)

Text message from: Hillary Clinton, Secretary of State

HBomb: meeting w/ china's premiere 2day on trade issues

BarackO: whats your strategy?

HBomb: not sure, uphill battle

BarackO: just do what u did in campaign

HBomb: ??

BarackO: drag it out like a Grateful Dead encore

FROM: Amazon.com
TO: Barack Obama
SUBJECT: Your Order Has Shipped

Greetings from Amazon.com. The following books have been shipped to you:

You: Being President

What to Expect When You're Expecting a Portuguese Water Dog

"Mr. Bojangles": My Wacky Life in Politics by Kim Jong-il

Jay Leno's Big Book of Mother-in-Law Jokes, Vol. III

Thank you for shopping with us.

FROM: Alan Greenspan
TO: Barack Obama
SUBJECT: Your Financial Future

Mr. President,

I hope this missive finds you well. I am enjoying being retired and exploring new opportunities.

Hey: How would you like to make up to $800 a week FROM YOUR OWN HOME, just by helping your friends and family save money on things that they already buy? One of my favorite products is the Shampoonagé hair-care system, which leaves my hair and scalp healthy, vibrant and rejuvenated.

Call me. You won't regret it,

Alan "Future Double Diamond" Greenspan

Top Three, Shampoonagé sales, Northeast Region

a.greenspan777@amway.com

Text message from: Robert Gates, Secretary of Defense

PearlyGates: hey. just googled "presidential line of succession"

BarackO: yeah?

PearlyGates: i'm number 6

BarackO: not bad

PearlyGates: u know who's ahead of me?

BarackO: have to go back and look . . .

PearlyGates: geithner

BarackO: yeah, well . . .

PearlyGates: geithner?!? seriously?!

BarackO: walk it off

FROM: NYTimes.com
TO: Barack Obama
SUBJECT: My Alerts: Articles in the New York Times containing the terms "Obama" **and** "sexy master statesman"

June 7, 2009 Compiled: 1:47 AM
U.S. / POLITICS

There was one article containing the terms **"Obama"** and **"sexy master statesman"**

Spurned by Obama, Sexy Master Statesman Leaps from Bridge

(NYT)

Otmar Hasler, the Prime Minister of one of the world's tiniest countries, Liechtenstein, jumped from a bridge yesterday after Barack Obama refused to return his emails. Since the bridges in Liechtenstein are also tiny, he was unhurt . . . (more)

FROM: George W. Bush
TO: Barack Obama
SUBJECT: Reflecting backwards

Dear Barack:

If I had some advice for you, it would just be to plunge into the sublime seas, dive deep and swim far, so you shall come back with self-respect, with new power, with an advanced experience that shall explain and overlook the old. I did this, and it helped big time.

Sincerely,
W

FROM: Barack Obama
TO: George W. Bush

Dear Mr. President:

Thank you. Isn't that Ralph Waldo Emerson?

Barack

FROM: George W. Bush
TO: Barack Obama

Barack,

Gotcha! Yeah, it was "Ralph" somebody. Turns out it's a breeze to do this on Laura's computer (press Ctrl+C on the part you want to fool somebody with, and then do Ctrl+V where you want to put it! Viola!)

Bye,
W

P.S. I sent Gore one by Moby Dick! He's gonna crap!

FROM: Congressman Dennis Kucinich
TO: Capitol Hill All Users Group
SUBJECT: Witnesses needed

Hi,

I was side-swiped by a black sedan with license plate "NRA4EVR" at the corner of 3rd Street and E. Capitol today at 4:05 p.m. Did anyone witness this? My Peace-clown suit is SHREDDED and my unicycle is basically totaled. That was my only form of transportation since Nader bought my bus.

Any details would be helpful.

P.S. is anyone interested in a Cockatoo? It's a little too intense for me. Will trade for fondue set.

FROM: Abraham Lincoln
TO: Barack Obama
SUBJECT: I Got to Third Base with Amelia Earhart!!!

Four score!

Best,
Abe

FROM: NYTimes
TO: Barack Obama
SUBJECT: My Alerts: Articles in the New York Times containing the terms "Obama" **and** "sexy master statesman"

June 13, 2009 Compiled: 1:47 AM
U.S. / POLITICS

There was one article containing the terms **"Obama"** and **"sexy master statesman"**

Obama vs. The Sexy Master Statesman: Ahmadinejad

(NYT)

Iranian President wows U.N. with new flare, cape, curly boots.

"He is definitely the new Obama," said Iceland's President Grímsson. "There is a sense that Barack is losing his . . . (more)

Text message from: Hillary Clinton

HBomb: meeting with G8 leaders 2day on trade issues

BarackO: your approach?

HBomb: still thinking about it

BarackO: do what u did in campaign

HBomb: drag it out too long?

BarackO: no. the other thing. boohoo, sniffle, sniffle, sob, sob

Text message to: Al Gore

BarackO: what's the diff btwn a seal and a sea lion?

NobelOscar07: dif't species. sea lions = larger + external ears and large hairless front flippers. why? new legislation?

BarackO: nope. just won $1000 off biden. he sez they r same animal.

FROM: Charles, Prince of Wales
TO: Barack Obama
SUBJECT: Question re: principalities

Just woke up this morning with the silliest
question: am I the Prince of America, too?

FROM: Barack Obama
TO: Prince Charles

Dear Prince Charles,

No. We're a democratic republic.

FROM: Prince Charles
TO: Barack Obama

Barack,

Of course. Everything got very tangled up during decolonization, you understand. One doesn't know what one is prince of anymore.

Is Canada right next door to you? Would you mind terribly asking them if I'm the prince of them?

Cheers,

HRH Prince Charles

FROM: Sarah Palin <Woof.Killa@ ChristUBetcha.gov>
TO: All U.S. Gov List
Subject: URGENT: THE PRINCESS IS A MAN!!!

Hello,

Many of you received the last email I sent that was hollerin' out to you regarding that Nigerian princess who had received a whole lotta money that she was too young to accept and due to the sexiest policies of that country and that economy of Africa, also.

After my wonderful husband Todd a snow-machine champion and I replied in giving our bank account numbers, it turns out that this princess is not a princess at all but a person, a man, hell bent on destroying America, hard working Americans such as Joe Six Pack, with regard to false asking for the money in that was that request.

I am ill about this position that we have been put in receiving such emails, and we have to be ever vigilant and also making sure that **never will we be exploited and taken advantage of that again by a FALSE PRINCESS that turns out to be a he.**

Please forward,
Sarah

FROM: Abraham Lincoln
TO: Barack Obama
SUBJECT: coming clean

Barack,

I want to apologize for the obnoxious tone of my previous emails.

I did not have sexual relations with those women (Amelia Earhart, Charlotte Bronte, or Marie Curie).

I was just trying to sound like a "ladies man." But that's not me. I have found someone very special to spend the rest of eternity with: Orville Wright.

And Wilbur Wright. Both.

I guess I just have a thing for pilots.

And dudes.

Peace,
Abe

Text message to: Joe Biden, Vice President

Barack0: need your help w/policy issue, Joe.

BidenMyTime: sure thing boss. shoot.

Barack0: what is feasibility of advancing disarmament talks w/other nations (i.e., beyond Russia)?

BidenMyTime: while the vast majority of **states** have adhered to the stipulations of the **Nuclear Nonproliferation Treaty,** a few states have either refused to sign the treaty or have pursued **nuclear weapons programs** while not being members of the treaty.

Barack0: did u just cut and paste from wikipedia?

Barack0: joe?

BidenMyTime: on amtrak, goin into tunnel, gonna lose u.

Barack Obama's Facebook Friend Updates

Sarah Palin can't wait to stir-fry a bear cub 2night

Hillary Clinton is blowing smoke up the Chinese's a&$#s

Ann Coulter just ordered another Appletini at TGIF's

George W. Bush is weedwhackin' his truck

Al Gore just polished his Emmy

Rush Limbaugh took the **"What Beer Are You?"** quiz with the result **Vicodin**

Sasha Obama is playing Castle Wolfenstein

Joe Biden is at Burlington Coat Factory

Dick Cheney is water-boarding at Lake Tahoe!

The Dalai Lama is

Text message from: Angelina Jolie

PittStop2: heard madonna wants to adopt yr aunt

BarackO: not gonna happen.

PittStop2: thank god! madonna's kind of a mess

BarackO: k

PittStop2: . . . and brad & I have LOTS more room than her

FROM: Gordon Brown, Prime Minister of The United Kingdom
TO: Barack Obama
SUBJECT: Idea!

Dear Mr. President,

What would you say to the idea of swapping jobs? I'd be the President of the United States and you'd be the British Prime Minister. You would love this job: this country's easy because they have a Queen. Some days I don't even go in.

For my part, it's not that I want to meet Martha Stewart, not at all. I just like America, and would like a chance to be her leader. By "her" I mean America, not Martha Stewart. Indeed I suspect that Martha will never be tamed by any man, certainly not

Gordon Brown. Does Martha ride horseback at all, by the way? God, there's an image for you.

Alas, it's late, I'm rat-arsed and blubbering on.

Cheers,
Gordon

Text message from: Hillary Clinton, Secretary of State

HBomb: can i go to africa this wknd?

BarackO: sure, why?

HBomb: i wanna give bill some space

BarackO: ok

HBomb: he should get nobel instead of gore

BarackO: right. Is that you, bill?

HBomb: yeah

BarackO: where did you find hillary's cel phone?

HBomb: in her purse

BarackO: do the right thing, bill

HBomb: I will. I'll smash it. Thx.

FROM: Arnold Schwarzenegger
TO: Barack Obama
SUBJECT: My whereabouts

I am deep inside Pakistan, down to my last Red Bull. Bin Laden is so close I can taste it. I need you to send me a thong, some face paint, and some *Oui* or *Hustler* magazines from the 1970s (for bartering purposes only).

I hang-glide into Tora Bora tomorrow,

Arnold

Text message to: Timothy Geithner, Secretary of the Treasury

Barack0: hey timothy

ZeitGeit: hey

Barack0: what is plan re: T-bills?

ZeitGeit: we start over in Second Life; issue currency in there

Barack0: ?

ZeitGeit: online roleplayer community

Barack0: what about real world?

ZeitGeit: it's better in Second Life: economy stronger and I have washboard abs and two girlfriends and my own island

Barack0: other ideas?

ZeitGeit: drop the rate for goldpieces in World of Warcraft and go against the werewolves hard

FROM: YouTube Service
TO: ThePresident@us.gov
SUBJECT: Dick Cheney sent you a video:
Baby panda bear sneezing

Hey W,

This is ten times cuter than the one you sent me. You have to watch to the end: he starts to sneeze then falls asleep then OMG he wakes up by sneezing! OMG OMG OMG!!!

Don't you just wanna' hug EVERY BABY PANDA you see?!

Dick

FROM: Dick Cheney
TO: ThePresident@us.gov
SUBJECT: PLEASE DELETE MY LAST EMAIL
(Baby Panda Sneezing)

Dear President Obama,

I mistakenly sent a video to what is now your address. I will shoot a baby panda if you mention this to anyone.

Seriously,
Dick Cheney

FROM: Dmitry Medvedev, President of Russia
TO: All World Leaders
SUBJECT: I am President of Russia

Hey Guys!

Just wanted to say "Hi" and that I am
Russian President. Also, do any of you
have hats or jackets that say what you're
president of? Maybe if we order together we
can get group discount.

Sincerely,
Dmitry Medvedev
PRESIDENT OF RUSSIA

P.S. Thinking of gag gift for Putin: T-shirt that
says "I'm with him, the President" with arrow
pointing to me. Thoughts?

FROM: beet_it@beetpower.org
TO: Barack Obama
SUBJECT: We need to have a "beet n' meet"

Dear President Obama,

We applaud you for planting a garden at the White House, but we are devastated that there is no room for beets in your plot.

Let me remind you that the beet growers caucus was instrumental in getting you elected.

In addition to an apology, we invite you to pose as Mr. August in our Annual Beetcake Calendar. (This would be tastefully shot, with Chiogga beets covering the penis.)

We look forward to meeting with you,

Dale Clondore
Director
Beet Growers Coalition

Text message from: Silvio Berlusconi, Prime Minister of Italy

Berlusconi: Bravo Obama, you make-a da nice victory for presidento!

BarackO: Grazie, Silvio. Thx 4 the msg. Look 4wrd to wrkng with Italian gov't.

Berlusconi: I hava da follow-uppa question. *Seriamente*: what kinda sunatana lotion do you use-a to make-a your sunatana so magnifico?

BarackO: No lotion. 100% "naturale"

Berlusconi: *Bravissimo*! I love-a da Americans! Our countries gonna make-a love all nighta together.

BarackO: ?

Berlusconi: Ciao bello!

Text message from: Justice Clarence Thomas

JustClarence: heard u r playing hoops @ white house!

Barack0: u heard correctly

JustClarence: cool. u guys need a strong fwd?

Barack0: nope, we're good. feinstein is crashing the boards big-time

JustClarence: sounds fun

Barack0: it really is — lotsa fun.

JustClarence: need a ref?

Barack0: no thx — we call our own fouls

JustClarence: I could wear a bulldog costume and do trampoline dunks!!

Barack0: justice stevens is already doing that (and has own t-shirt launcher)

FROM: Facebook
TO: Barack Obama
SUBJECT: Joe Lieberman suggested you add a friend on Facebook . . .

Joe Lieberman recently became friends with Newt Gingrich and thinks you may know Newt, too.

Joe says, **"Check out Newt's 25 Random Things about Me (#5: I can do the splits)"**

Do you want to be friends with Newt Gingrich?

Thanks,
The Facebook Team

Text message from: Malia Obama

Malia: dad can i watch barney?

BarackO: aren't u too old for purple dino?

Malia: no, barney frank — on CSPAN

BarackO: depends, what is he saying?

Malia: dunno! he's just really funny

113

FROM: Ralph Nader
TO: Rahm Emanuel
CC: Barack Obama
SUBJECT: Czar Me?

What's up, bitches? Was wondering if there are any spots in the administration. I could do one of the czar jobs. Is there a seatbelt czar?

Ralph Nader

FROM: Rahm Emanuel
TO: Ralph Nader

Ralph,

Have you tried the Salvation Army? They are very crazy-friendly and you could get the employee discount on those F&@&!NG suits you like. L8R N8R.

Oh and,

F*^# YOU,

Rahm

FROM: Sidwell Friends School
TO: Barack Obama, Michelle Obama
SUBJECT: Sasha's Final Grades

Friendship:	A
Just Being Friends:	A
Making New Friends:	A
Getting Together with Old Friends:	A
Best Friends Forever:	A
Not Letting Friends Drink and Drive:	A

Sincerely,
Headmaster Nancy Miller

FROM: Osama Bin Laden <noreply@ KindOfNearToraBora.afg>
TO: Barack Obama
SUBJECT: will trade ceasefire for air conditioner + new norelco

. . . not really, but I would like to find a way to make this whole jihad thing less of a time-suck for me. I think I'm ready to pack it in, get a little condo, and find some frumpy good-hearted couch-face who can cook a shawarma.

Even a 9-hole course is murder on my knees (doc says its from bad arch support?). Plus, I want to work on my writing (*Hiking the Donkey Trails of Afghanistan,* and *Pakistan on a Budget and Dialysis.*)

Think about it, maybe give me a call?

I "might" be at the Hooters in Islamabad till Wednesday. Ask for "Tony."

I hate you guys,
Bin Laden

P.S. An old bodybuilder with saggy tits is wandering around the town square handing out *Oui* magazines. Did you have anything to do with this?

FROM: eBay
TO: Barack Obama
SUBJECT: Barack, an Item You Have Bid on is Ending Soon!!!

You are currently the high bidder on Item 987756238:

"You Can Have Arms like Michelle Obama in 30 Days!" (Workout DVD)

Seller: cathysjunkntreasures (77) (100%+)

Current Bid: $5.69

Own the best-selling workout DVD used by the NAVY SEALS.

FROM: Dr. Phil
TO: Barack Obama; Hillary Clinton
SUBJECT: Notes on last therapy session

Mr. President and Madame Secretary,

Our last session was fruitful. Hillary, you talked about the need to assert your identity while working for a "political pre-schooler." Barack, you mentioned your difficulty relying on someone whom you had previously regarded as a "duplicitous Lady-Grinch."

I think we're getting somewhere. Remember your homework (self-esteem quiz) for Tuesday,

Dr. Phil

P.S. Can we move this to TV? Major $$$ for everyone involved. I'm talking bailout-level money.

FROM: Barack Obama
TO: Mitt Romney
SUBJECT: Quiet Evening Alone?

I'm trying to get out of here "early" (aka 8:45 pm ☺). What would you think about just getting a bottle of merlot and watching "Big Love" or something? We don't have to talk about the Republicans, etc. — just relax and unwind.

B

FROM: Mitt Romney
TO: Barack Obama

You know, I am so relieved to get this email from you, sir. I would actually really enjoy that.

Mitt

FROM: Barack Obama
TO: Mitt Romney

Mitt,

Deepest apologies. That email was meant
for Michelle. The auto-fill on my email put in
"Mitt" when I typed "Mi —".

Again, my sincere regrets.

Take care,
Barack

FROM: Mitt Romney
TO: Barack Obama

Of course! I knew that ☺. Did you think my reply was pretty funny? I thought it was funny!

See you later, LOL,

Mitt

Text message from:
Barbara Boxer, Senator (D-CA)

HotBoxer: hey, watcha doin?

BarackO: writing speech

HotBoxer: u goin 2nite?

BarackO: 2 what?

HotBoxer: kegger and phish cover band ☺

BarackO: who's goin?

HotBoxer: me, pelosi, stinky, j. kerry ☹, muskrat and toolbox

BarackO: gotta work

HotBoxer: kucinich is bringing didgeridoo

BarackO: meh. send pics

124

FROM: Bobby Jindal, Governor of Louisiana
TO: Barack Obama
SUBJECT: Plan for Personal Excellence

Dear Mr. President,

Who's your life coach? Also, is there a particular public-speaking video that you could recommend?

Sincerely,
Bobby

FROM: Barack Obama
TO: Bobby Jindal

Dear Gov. Jindal,

"If you even dream of beating me you'd better wake up and apologize."

— Muhammad Ali

Barack

Text message from: Michelle Obama

FirstLady2U: u looked cute on CNN ☺

BarackO: really? ☺

FirstLady2U: can u get away for 15 min.'s? ☺

BarackO: YES I CAN ☺

FirstLady2U: good, cuz Bo barfed in west wing. needs 2 be cleaned up ☹

FROM: Pastor Rick Warren
TO: Barack Obama
SUBJECT: Need me for any other big prayers coming up?

Hey,

Thanks again for letting me do the prayer at the inauguration. Beats the hell out of selling waterbeds! Sorry for pulling out all that Yeshua, Jehovah, Shazaam stuff. At least I didn't speak in tongues! Blbablabyaghblabharlytaha! LOL ☺

Anyhoo, do you need me for any other big events coming up? I could do my "Escape from Brokeback Mountain" sermon for the Easter Egg hunt?

Lemme know,
Pastor Rick

FROM: Barack Obama
TO: Northern California Renaissance Faire
SUBJECT: I'm coming to Renn Faire!

Hello,

Just writing to confirm my attendance at Renn Faire again this year. I know things are different since the election, so I've taken measures to ensure that my presence will not disrupt the faire:

I will be disguised as either Sir Lancelot (with real chainmail) or a Druid Sorcerer (w/ tabard, cummerbund, and mask). My Secret Service detail will be dressed as: Renaissance Village Men, Sea Wenches, and Peters Pans.

Starting at promptly 0900, I will wander around, drink some mead, try my hand at glass-blowing, and join a mandolin jam. At 1300 I will partake of a merry feast of turkey legs with pumpernickel loaf and then disembark on Air Force One, which will be disguised as a pirate frigate.

Yea we canne,
Oswyn, Lord of Avendor (Barack Obama)

Text message from: Russian Prime Minister Vladimir Putin

RazzPutin: hey Barack

Barack0: hey putin

RazzPutin: u know what is best vodka?

Barack0: no, what?

RazzPutin: is vodka that pretty girl buy u

Barack0: LOL, pretty funny

RazzPutin: u know best kind of borscht?

Barack0: super busy, but what?

RazzPutin: is borscht your mother-in-law have to make . . .

RazzPutin: . . . at gunpoint of AK-47! LOL

Barack0: c ya

RazzPutin: u know what is best kind of sheep hat?

Barack0: can't talk now

RazzPutin: is one that's not b-a-a-a-a-a-a-d

FROM: Depts. of Transportation, Housing and Urban Development
TO: Barack Obama
SUBJECT: What does "green infrastructure" mean?

I think we blew it really, really bad. We have just been painting everything green: bridges, highways, power plants, trucks, dams, housing projects . . . Please tell me this is what you meant by creating a green infrastructure. We're gonna lose our jobs, right?

Shaun and Ray,
Sec'tys of HUD and DOT

FROM: Michael Steele, Chairman, Republican National Committee (RNC)
TO: All U.S. Gov List; Republican National Committee
SUBJECT: Off the hook!

Hello All,

More ideas for bringing hip hop into the Republican Party:

I will be changing my name to "MC Stainless." If we're going to do this right, I suggest some of you other conservative leaders also change your names. Below are some suggestions:

Rush Limbaugh — Phat Shady

Gov. Bobby Jindal — MC Freaky Ji-Bo

John McCain — Ole Creepy Bastard

House Republican Leader John Boehner — Da' Boehn Yard

Schwarzenegger — The Termi-traitor

Matt Drudge — (no change, already sounds like a rap name)

Ann Coulter — MC Skeletor

Joe Lieberman — Deez Nutz

Let's do this!

MC Stainless (formerly Michael Steele)

FROM: Barack Obama
TO: Executive Branch IT Dept.
SUBJECT: No I can't

Look: You guys are gonna kill me, but I can't deal with this BlackBerry anymore.

Please shut it down.

I know,
You told me so,

Barack

P.S. I'm gonna check my email one more time — give me 5 minutes. 10 minutes. Actually, let's do it tomorrow morning — I'll send you a final email to confirm.

Authors' Note

This book is fiction. None of the correspondence within it is real. It is definitely not intended to inform domestic or foreign policy.

Illustration Credits

Acknwldgmnts

TO: our agnt danielle svetcov + levine greenberg lit agency: u guys r awesome — srsly — thank u

TO: john parsley @ LB: gr8 2 wrk w/u ag8n. THNQ 4 XLNT 8dting

TO: r friends who read drfts: THX! — r u mad that we did not listn 2 yr notes? Srry ☹ — ran out of time!

TO: r families: THNQ + we luv u :-*

TO: pres. BarackO: PLS txt us back; we want 2 talk 2 u!!!

CU L8R,

KH

About the Authors

Lisa Keating

Kasper Hauser is (L to R) Dan Klein, James Reichmuth, John Reichmuth, and Rob Baedeker. They are the authors of *Weddings of the* Times (a parody of the *New York Times* wedding pages) and *SkyMaul: Happy Crap You Can Buy from a Plane*. The group's members have written for HBO Digital and appeared on Comedy Central, and their work has been featured on *This American Life*. They are based in San Francisco.

Information about their award-winning live shows and podcasts can be found at www.kasperhauser.com.